WHO'S A GOOD DOG?

A KEEPSAKE MEMORY BOOK FOR MY DOG

ASTRA BERZINSKAS

CASTLE POINT BOOKS

NEW YORK

WHO'S A GOOD DOG. Copyright © 2020 by St. Martin's Press.
All rights reserved. Printed in Singapore. For information,
address St. Martin's Press, 120 Broadway, New York, NY 10271.

www.castlepointbooks.com

The Castle Point Books trademark is owned by Castle Point Publishing, LLC.
Castle Point books are published and distributed by St. Martin's Press.

ISBN 978-1-250- 27061-0 (hardcover)

Design by Tara Long
Composition by Noora Cox

Our books may be purchased in bulk for promotional, educational, or business use.
Please contact your local bookseller or the Macmillan Corporate and
Premium Sales Department at 1-800-221-7945, extension 5442,
or by email at MacmillanSpecialMarkets@macmillan.com.

First Edition: June 2020

10 9 8 7 6 5 4 3 2 1

THIS BOOK BELONGS TO

- -

PROUD OWNER OF

- -

CONTENTS

HOME

IS WHERE

THE DOG IS

INTRODUCTION

YOUR LIFE JUST WOULDN'T BE THE SAME WITHOUT YOUR SWEET PUP. Having that furry wonder in your life fills your days with an extra dose of joy, playtime, inspiration, and love. Pay tribute to everything you adore about your canine companion in *Who's a Good Dog*, a keepsake journal for devoted dog owners like you. Collect your memories and photos all in one place and tell the story of how your four-legged family member wiggled and wagged and woofed his or her way into your heart. Whether it's a frolicking puppy that loves you unconditionally, an adult pet that makes your house a home, or a loyal senior who still greets you excitedly at the door, this journal offers a chance to express your appreciation for the dog in your life and create a keepsake to make memories last forever.

NO PUP LIKE MY PUP

WHAT WAS YOUR EXPERIENCE WITH DOGS
BEFORE MEETING YOUR CURRENT PUP?

- -

- -

- -

- -

- -

Where did you find your dog?

A) BREEDER

B) SHELTER

C) RESCUE ORGANIZATION

D) OTHER -

WHAT BREED (OR BREEDS) IS YOUR DOG?

WHAT DID YOU KNOW ABOUT YOUR DOG
BEFORE YOU CHOSE HIM OR HER?

WHAT HAVE YOU SINCE LEARNED ABOUT HIM OR HER?

DESCRIBE THE MOMENT WHEN YOU FIRST MET YOUR DOG.

_____

_____

_____

_____

ADD A PHOTO OF THAT SPECIAL DAY BELOW:

HOW HAS YOUR LIFE CHANGED SINCE MEETING YOUR DOG?

[**DOGS ARE NOT OUR WHOLE LIFE,
BUT THEY MAKE OUR LIVES WHOLE.**
—ROGER CARAS]

WHAT MADE YOU CHOOSE YOUR DOG ABOVE ALL OTHERS?

WHAT QUALITIES DID YOU LOVE ABOUT HIM OR HER FROM THE START?

TELL THE STORY BEHIND YOUR DOG'S NAME.

What nicknames or terms of endearment do you have for him or her?

_____

_____

_____

_____

_____

WHAT WAS IT LIKE WHEN YOU
FIRST BROUGHT YOUR DOG HOME?

_____

_____

_____

_____

_____

WHERE DID YOUR PUP SLEEP THE FIRST NIGHT?

WHERE DOES YOUR PUP LIKE TO SLEEP NOW?

WHO WERE YOUR DOG'S FIRST DOG FRIENDS?

WHO ARE YOUR DOG'S BEST DOG FRIENDS NOW?

WHAT WAS ONE OF THE FIRST TRICKS OR SKILLS
YOU TAUGHT YOUR DOG?

LIST ALL THE THINGS YOUR DOG
HAS LEARNED TO DO SINCE THAT DAY:

WHAT SURPRISED YOU ABOUT YOUR DOG?

WHEN HAVE YOU BEEN MOST PROUD OF YOUR DOG?

What three words would you use
to describe your pup's personality?

WHEN DOES YOUR DOG SEEM HAPPIEST?

What sounds always make his or her ears perk up?

WHAT WAS THE LAST THING THAT
GOT YOUR DOG'S TAIL WAGGING?

WHO ARE YOUR DOG'S FAVORITE HUMAN VISITORS?

Which family members, friends,
or neighbors adore your dog most?

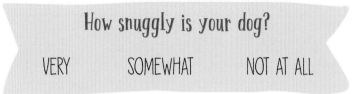

How snuggly is your dog?

VERY   SOMEWHAT   NOT AT ALL

HOW DOES YOUR DOG SHOW HIS OR HER LOVE?

_____

_____

_____

Which does your dog enjoy most?

BELLY RUBS   GENTLE PATS

BIG HUGS   BUTT SCRATCHES

OTHER:

_____

ADD A PHOTO OF YOUR DOG LOOKING HAPPY:

A DOG IS THE ONLY THING
ON EARTH THAT LOVES YOU
MORE THAN HE LOVES HIMSELF.

—JOSH BILLINGS

WHEN HAS YOUR DOG MADE YOU LAUGH
WHEN YOU REALLY NEEDED IT?

DESCRIBE THE BOND YOU HAVE WITH YOUR DOG.

HAPPY
BIRTHDAY
TO
YOU

HOW DO YOU USUALLY CELEBRATE IT?

HOW HAS YOUR DOG GROWN OR CHANGED SINCE PUPPYHOOD?

ATTACH A PHOTO OF YOUR PUP ON HIS OR HER BIRTHDAY:

CLOWNING AROUND

WHAT IS THE GOOFIEST THING YOUR DOG DOES?

_____

_____

_____

ADD A PHOTO OF YOUR DOG BEING A GOOFBALL:

LIST THE TOP 5 THINGS YOU ENJOY DOING WITH YOUR DOG:

1. _____
2. _____
3. _____
4. _____
5. _____

LIST YOUR DOG'S TOP 3 FAVORITE TOYS:

1. _____
2. _____
3. _____

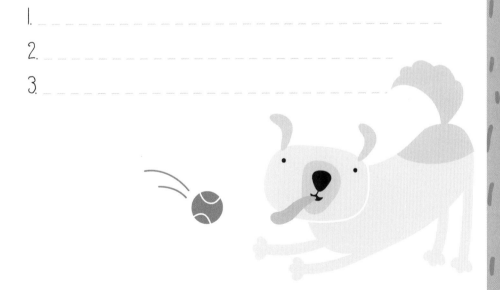

DESCRIBE SOMETHING ONLY YOU KNOW ABOUT YOUR DOG.

_____

_____

_____

What games do you play with your dog?

_____

_____

_____

WHAT ALWAYS MAKES YOUR DOG'S TAIL WAG?

_____

_____

_____

IT IS AMAZING
HOW MUCH LOVE
AND LAUGHTER
[DOGS] BRING INTO
OUR LIVES AND EVEN
HOW MUCH CLOSER
WE BECOME WITH
EACH OTHER
BECAUSE OF THEM.

—JOHN GROGAN

What is your dog's personality type at home?

RESERVED AND SHY

LIFE OF THE PARTY

GOES WITH THE FLOW

What is your dog's personality type at a dog park or in a social setting?

RESERVED AND SHY

LIFE OF THE PARTY

GOES WITH THE FLOW

WHAT IS MOST REMARKABLE OR ADORABLE
ABOUT YOUR DOG'S APPEARANCE?

SKETCH YOUR LOVEABLE PUP IN THE SPACE BELOW.

YOU CANNOT SHARE
YOUR LIFE WITH A DOG...
AND NOT KNOW PERFECTLY
WELL THAT ANIMALS HAVE
PERSONALITIES AND MINDS
AND FEELINGS.

—JANE GOODALL

WHAT SONG EXPRESSES YOUR DOG'S SPIRIT BEST?

_____

_____

_____

IF YOU HAD TO GUESS WHO YOUR DOG WAS IN A PAST LIFE,
WHAT WOULD YOU GUESS?

_____

_____

_____

_____

Finish this silly limerick about your dog:

THERE ONCE WAS A DOG FROM _____

WHO _____ .

_____ ,

_____ ,

_____ .

Style Hound

What accessories or costumes has your dog been known to wear?

ADD A PHOTO OF YOUR DOG SHOWING OFF
HIS OR HER UNIQUE STYLE BELOW:

THE GREAT PLEASURE
OF A DOG IS THAT YOU
MAY MAKE A FOOL OF
YOURSELF WITH HIM,
AND NOT ONLY WILL
HE NOT SCOLD YOU,
BUT HE WILL MAKE A
FOOL OF HIMSELF, TOO.

—SAMUEL BUTLER

WHO HAS YOUR DOG WON OVER WITH HIS CUTENESS?

What personality trait(s) do you share with your dog?

WHEN HAS YOUR DOG GOTTEN INTO TROUBLE?

ADD A PHOTO OF YOUR DOG CAUGHT DOING SOMETHING
HE OR SHE IS NOT SUPPOSED TO DO:

CANINE ADVENTURES

HOW DOES YOUR DOG "ASK" FOR A WALK OR TO BE LET OUTSIDE?

_____

_____

_____

_____

_____

How does your dog react when you get out the leash?

_____

_____

_____

_____

What's your dog's on-leash personality?

A) STOPS TO SNIFF EVERY BLADE OF GRASS

B) PULLS YOU EVERY WHICH WAY

C) STEADY TROT BY YOUR SIDE

D) OTHER _____

What's your dog's off-leash personality?

A) STICKS CLOSE BY YOU

B) WANDERS OFF, BUT CHECKS IN

C) RUNS AS FAST AND FAR AS POSSIBLE

D) OTHER _____

What "look" does your
dog often give you?

DOGS DO SPEAK,
BUT ONLY TO
THOSE WHO KNOW
HOW TO LISTEN.

—ORHAN PAMUK

Have Dog, Will Travel

ON A SCALE OF 1 TO 10,
HOW MUCH DOES YOUR DOG ENJOY CAR RIDES?

1 2 3 4 5 6 7 8 9 10

HOW WELL DOES YOUR DOG BEHAVE ON CAR RIDES?

Which other modes of transportation has your pup tried?

PUPPY STROLLER
BICYCLE TRAILER OR BASKET
SUBWAY
BUS
TRAIN
AIRPLANE

ADD A PHOTO OF YOUR DOG ON THE GO HERE:

Travel Log

MAKE A LIST BELOW OF ALL THE PLACES YOUR DOG HAS TRAVELED:

WHAT ARE YOUR FAVORITE
DOG-FRIENDLY HOTELS?

----

*What place of business
do you wish was more
dog friendly?*

WHAT ARE YOUR FAVORITE DOG-FRIENDLY CAFÉS OR RESTAURANTS?

LIST 3 NEW EXPERIENCES YOU'D LIKE YOUR DOG TO HAVE:

1. ....
2. ....
3. ....

LIST 3 PLACES YOU'D LIKE TO TRAVEL WITH YOUR DOG:

1. ....
2. ....
3. ....

Add a photo of your latest adventure together:

THE JOURNEY OF LIFE IS SWEETER WHEN TRAVELED WITH A DOG.

—BRIDGET WILLOUGHBY

HOW WELL DOES YOUR DOG BEHAVE IN PUBLIC?

HAVE YOU EVER BROUGHT YOUR DOG TO WORK, OR WANTED TO?
HOW DO YOU THINK IT WOULD GO?

What is the most interesting or unexpected place you took your dog?

What is the last public event or place you visited with your dog?

ALL MY DOGS HAVE BEEN
SCAMPS AND THIEVES AND
TROUBLEMAKERS AND I'VE
ADORED THEM ALL.

—HELEN HAYES

TOP DOG

Best in Show

IF YOU ENTERED YOUR DOG IN A SHOW, WHICH
CATEGORY WOULD SUIT HIM OR HER BEST?

○ SPORTING GROUP
○ HOUND GROUP
○ WORKING GROUP
○ TERRIER GROUP
○ TOY GROUP
○ NON-SPORTING GROUP
○ HERDING GROUP
○ A COMBINATION OF _____ AND _____
○ OTHER: _____

How do you think your dog would do?

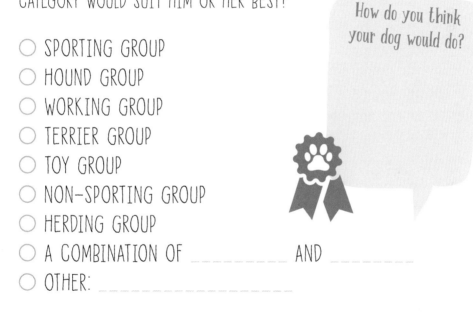

WHAT WOULD YOU LOVE TO SHOW OFF ABOUT YOUR DOG?

_____

_____

WHICH OF YOUR DOG'S QUALITIES ARE
COMMON FOR ITS BREED(S)?

WHICH OF YOUR DOG'S QUALITIES ARE
UNCOMMON FOR ITS BREED(S)?

WHAT BEHAVIORS, IF ANY, MIGHT GET YOUR DOG DISQUALIFIED?

If there were a talent portion, what
would your dog perform?

Hollywood Hound

IF YOUR DOG WERE IN A MOVIE,
WHAT ROLE WOULD SUIT HIM OR HER BEST?

A) ACTION HERO

B) PUPPY IN DISTRESS

C) HEARTTHROB

D) PESKY VILLAIN

E) GOOFY SIDEKICK

HOW WOULD THE DIRECTOR DESCRIBE YOUR DOG?

A) A WALK IN THE PARK

B) A WORK IN PROGRESS

C) A TOTAL DOGGY DIVA

What items would your dog want
sent to his or her trailer?

ADD A GLAMOROUS CLOSE-UP OR
DRAMATIC HEADSHOT OF YOUR DOG HERE:

DOGS GOT PERSONALITY.
PERSONALITY GOES
A LONG WAY.

—QUENTIN TARANTINO

Making the Grade

GIVE YOUR DOG A GRADE FROM A TO F
IN THE FOLLOWING CATEGORIES.

Subject	Grade
LOVABILITY	
FRESH BREATH	
LEASH WALKING	
COMPANIONSHIP	
LISTENING SKILLS	
CHARM	
INTELLIGENCE	
EAGERNESS TO PLEASE	
SENSE OF HUMOR	
FRIENDLINESS	

Progress Report

WHAT SKILLS IS YOUR DOG STILL LEARNING?

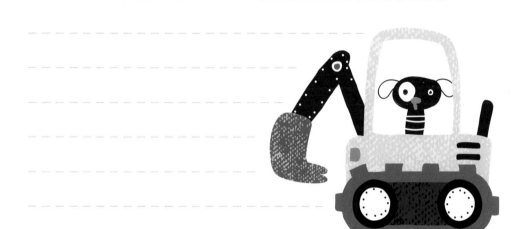

WHAT SKILLS ARE YOU STILL LEARNING AS AN OWNER?

CHOW HOUND

HOW FOOD FOCUSED IS YOUR DOG?

A) MY DOG LIVES FOR FOOD.

B) MY DOG LIKES FOOD.

C) MY DOG EATS TO STAY ALIVE.

What dog treats are his or her favorite?

_____

_____

_____

_____

WHAT HUMAN FOODS DOES YOUR DOG GO CRAZY FOR?

IF A DOG'S PRAYERS WERE ANSWERED,
BONES WOULD RAIN FROM THE SKY.

—PROVERB

A DOG DESIRES
AFFECTION MORE
THAN ITS DINNER.
WELL—ALMOST.

—CHARLOTTE GRAY

WHAT IS YOUR DOG'S MAIN DIET?

- -

- -

- -

- -

What food hang-ups does your dog have?

How eager is your dog at mealtime?

A) MY DOG INHALES HIS OR HER FOOD.

B) MY DOG EATS WHEN HE OR SHE IS READY.

C) MY DOG BARELY SEEMS TO NOTICE HIS OR HER FOOD.

How would you describe your dog's "table manners"?

A) NEAT AND TIDY

B) COULD USE A NAPKIN

C) SLOBBER CITY

WHAT TRICKS WILL YOUR DOG DO FOR HIS OR HER FAVORITE TREAT?

WHAT NONFOOD ITEMS HAS YOUR DOG
BEEN KNOWN TO EAT OR CHEW?

HOW DOES YOUR DOG LET YOU KNOW WHEN HE OR SHE IS HUNGRY?

What does your dog refuse to eat?

WHEN HAS YOUR DOG EATEN SOMETHING
HE OR SHE WASN'T SUPPOSED TO?

How successful at begging is your dog?

ADD A PHOTO OF HIS OR HER BEST "PUPPY DOG EYES" HERE:

How would you describe your dog's build?

A) LEAN AND MUSCULAR
B) A LITTLE SQUISHY
C) EXTRA FLUFFY
D) PLEASANTLY PLUMP

WHO, IN YOUR FAMILY OR CIRCLE OF FRIENDS,
HAS BEEN KNOWN TO SLIP YOUR DOG TABLE SCRAPS?

WHAT TRUSTY TREATS NEVER FAIL TO HIDE YOUR DOG'S MEDICINE?

IF YOU THINK DOGS CAN'T
COUNT, TRY PUTTING THREE
DOG BISCUITS IN YOUR
POCKET AND THEN GIVING
FIDO ONLY TWO OF THEM.

—PHIL PASTORET

RANK THESE HUMAN TREATS FROM 1 *(MAXIMUM DROOL)*
TO 5 *(MINIMUM DROOL)* ON BEHALF OF YOUR DOG.

_____ PEANUT BUTTER

_____ CHEESE

_____ BACON

_____ HOT DOG

_____ STEAK BONE

Who enjoys food more,
you or your dog?

HOW PROTECTIVE IS YOUR DOG OF HIS OR HER FOOD ON A SCALE FROM
1 *(MY FOOD IS YOUR FOOD)* TO 10 *(DON'T THINK I WON'T BITE YOU)*?

1 2 3 4 5 6 7 8 9 10

WHAT FOODS DO YOU LOVE TO SHARE WITH YOUR DOG?

ADD A PHOTO OF YOUR DOG CHOWING DOWN HERE:

FURRY AND FIT

HOW FIT IS YOUR DOG?

_____

_____

_____

HOW STRONG IS YOUR DOG?

_____

_____

_____

Just the Facts

HOW TALL IS YOUR DOG ON ALL FOURS?

HOW TALL IS YOUR DOG STANDING ON ITS HIND LEGS?

HOW LONG IS YOUR DOG FROM NOSE TO TAIL?

HOW MUCH DOES YOUR DOG WEIGH?

WHAT SPORT WOULD YOUR DOG PLAY IF HE OR SHE COULD? WHY?

WHAT DOES YOUR DOG LIKE TO CHASE?

WHEN HAVE YOU HAD TO CHASE AFTER YOUR DOG?

RATE YOUR DOG'S JUMPING SKILLS ON A SCALE FROM
PAWS OF LEAD (1) TO *GRAVITY DEFYING* (10).

1   2   3   4   5   6   7   8   9   10

THE DOG WAS CREATED
SPECIALLY FOR CHILDREN.
HE IS A GOD OF FROLIC.

—HENRY WARD BEECHER

ADD A PHOTO OF YOU ON A WALK OR HIKE WITH YOUR DOG HERE:

How many times do you walk your dog each day?

What is your dog's idea of a good walk?

A) A MARATHON

B) A JAUNT AROUND THE NEIGHBORHOOD

C) A QUICK TRIP UP THE ROAD AND BACK

D) A SLOW MOSEY TO THE FOOD DISH

HAVE YOU EVER GONE HIKING WITH YOUR DOG?
DESCRIBE THE EXPERIENCE HERE:

_____

_____

_____

_____

DESCRIBE THE LAST TIME YOUR DOG VISITED
A LAKE, RIVER, OR OCEAN:

How well can your
dog swim?

Rover to the Rescue

IF YOU WERE EVER INJURED OR NEEDED HELP, HOW
MIGHT YOUR DOG TRY TO RESCUE YOU? EXPLAIN.

Dirty Dog

AFTER A GOOD PLAY SESSION OUTSIDE, HOW DIRTY IS YOUR DOG?

ADD A PHOTO OF YOUR DIRTY DOG HERE:

DAPPER DOG

WHERE AND HOW OFTEN DOES YOUR DOG GET GROOMED?

_____

_____

_____

_____

_____

How does your dog feel about baths?

HAPPINESS IS A WARM PUPPY.
–CHARLES SHULTZ

Add a photo of your well-groomed pup here:

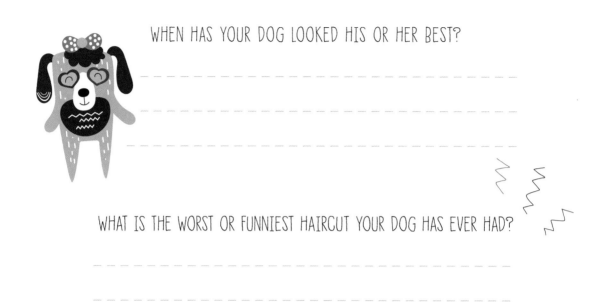

WHEN HAS YOUR DOG LOOKED HIS OR HER BEST?

- -

- -

- -

WHAT IS THE WORST OR FUNNIEST HAIRCUT YOUR DOG HAS EVER HAD?

- -

- -

Attach a photo of your dog's face here:

DRAW ON A HAT, A MOUSTACHE, A MOHAWK, OR ANYTHING ELSE THAT
COMES TO MIND AND GIVE HIM OR HER A WHOLE NEW LOOK!

IF YOU ARE A DOG
AND YOUR OWNER
SUGGESTS THAT YOU
WEAR A SWEATER...
SUGGEST THAT HE
WEAR A TAIL.

—FRAN LEBOWITZ

THE CALL OF THE WILD

HOW GOOD IS YOUR DOG AT SNIFFING OUT FOOD?

HOW GOOD IS YOUR DOG AT SPOTTING
A SQUIRREL OR BUNNY FROM AFAR?

What instincts are strongest in your dog?

WHAT CAN YOUR DOG DO BETTER THAN YOU?

ADD A PHOTO OF YOUR DOG DOING WHAT HE OR SHE DOES BEST:

Howls and Growls

WHAT SOUNDS DOES YOUR DOG OFTEN MAKE?

....

....

....

....

....

What gets him or her howling or barking?

CAN YOUR DOG "SING" ALONG TO MUSIC? IF SO,
WHAT KIND IS HIS OR HER FAVORITE?

THE POOR DOG, IN LIFE
THE FIRMEST FRIEND,
THE FIRST TO WELCOME,
FOREMOST TO DEFEND.

−LORD BYRON

HOW GOOD OF A WATCHDOG IS YOUR PUP?

GIVE AN EXAMPLE OF A TIME WHEN YOUR
DOG WAS PROTECTIVE OF YOU.

WHICH INSTINCTIVE REACTION IS MORE LIKELY IN YOUR DOG?
(CIRCLE ONE)

fight   flight

At what does your dog growl?

_____

_____

_____

WHAT PEOPLE OR ANIMALS SCARE YOUR DOG MOST?

_____

_____

WHAT SOUNDS SCARE YOUR DOG?

_____

_____

_____

_____

THE GREATEST FEAR DOGS KNOW IS THE FEAR THAT YOU WILL NOT COME BACK WHEN YOU GO OUT THE DOOR WITHOUT THEM.

—STANLEY COREN

PACK MENTALITY

WOULD YOU DESCRIBE YOUR DOG AS A LEADER OR FOLLOWER?

WHAT KINDS OF DOGS DOES YOUR DOG GET ALONG WITH BEST?

WHAT OTHER ANIMALS DOES YOUR DOG GET ALONG WITH?

ADD A PHOTO OF YOUR DOG WITH AN ANIMAL FRIEND HERE:

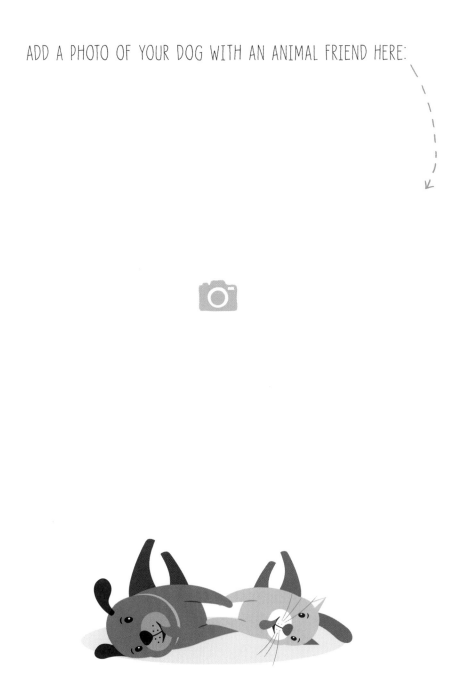

WHAT TOYS OR COMFORTS HELP YOUR DOG PASS
THE TIME WHEN HE OR SHE IS HOME ALONE?

_____

_____

_____

_____

How can you tell when your dog
needs love or attention?

_____

_____

_____

_____

_____

To whom in your family is your dog most attached?

IN WHAT WAY DOES YOUR DOG COMPLETE YOUR FAMILY?

_____

_____

_____

_____

A DOG TEACHES
A BOY FIDELITY,
PERSEVERANCE,
AND TO TURN
AROUND THREE
TIMES BEFORE
LYING DOWN.

—ROBERT BENCHLEY

WHAT LESSONS HAVE YOU LEARNED FROM YOUR DOG?

How does your dog know that he or she can count on you?

HEAD OF THE CLASS

What commands does your dog know? Circle them below.

SIT   DOWN

STAY   COME

HEEL   DROP IT

OTHER: _ _ _ _ _ _ _ _ _ _ _ _ _ _ _

How did you train your dog? Circle all that apply.

PROFESSIONAL TRAINER   GROUP CLASS

BOOKS   VIDEOS

I JUST WINGED IT

HOW WELL DOES YOUR DOG LEARN?

ℓℓℓℓℓℓ

WHAT HELPS HIM OR HER LEARN?

ℓℓℓℓℓℓ

WHAT COMMANDS DO YOU WISH HE OR SHE KNEW BETTER?

THERE'S NO REASON TO
KEEP A PIECE OF FURNITURE
IN YOUR HOUSE THAT IS SO
SACRED AND RARE THAT
YOU CAN'T PUT YOUR FEET
UP ON IT AND A DOG CAN'T
JUMP UP ON IT.

—ELIZABETH GILBERT

HOW PATIENT ARE YOU AS A TRAINER?

Who is most patient with your dog?

Who does your dog seem to respect most?

HOW OBEDIENT IS YOUR DOG ON A SCALE FROM
1 (YOUR WISH IS MY COMMAND) TO 10 (YOU'RE NOT THE BOSS OF ME)?

1   2   3   4   5   6   7   8   9   10

HOW DO YOU REWARD YOUR DOG WHEN
HE OR SHE IS BEING ESPECIALLY GOOD?

- -

- -

- -

- -

WHAT IS THE NICEST THING ANYONE HAS SAID ABOUT YOUR DOG?

- -

- -

- -

A DOG CAN SHOW
YOU MORE HONEST
AFFECTION WITH A
FLICK OF HIS TAIL THAN
A MAN CAN GATHER
THROUGH A LIFETIME
OF HANDSHAKES.

—GENE HILL

ADD A PHOTO OF YOUR DOG PERFORMING
HIS OR HER BEST TRICK HERE:

DOGS HAVE GIVEN US
THEIR ABSOLUTE ALL...
THEY SERVE US IN
RETURN FOR SCRAPS.
IT IS WITHOUT A DOUBT
THE BEST DEAL MAN
HAS EVER MADE.

—ROGER CARAS

HEALTHY HOUND

HOW HEALTHY IS YOUR DOG FOR HIS OR HER AGE?

What is the first sign that your dog isn't feeling well?

WHEN HAVE YOU EVER BEEN CONCERNED ABOUT YOUR DOG'S HEALTH?

WHAT MAKES YOUR DOG FEEL HIS OR HER BEST?

WHAT DO YOU DO TO KEEP YOUR DOG HEALTHY AND HAPPY?

WHAT DOES YOUR DOG DO TO KEEP *YOU* HEALTHY AND HAPPY?

Tell your dog why he or she is a good dog
in the space below.

THE WORLD WOULD
BE A NICER PLACE
IF EVERYONE HAD
THE ABILITY TO LOVE
AS UNCONDITIONALLY
AS A DOG.

—M. K. CLINTON

DOGS LEAVE
LITTLE PAWPRINTS
ON OUR HEARTS.

Paws to Appreciate Your Dog

CREATE A PAW-SOME KEEPSAKE OF YOUR DOG.
GENTLY PAINT THE PAD OF YOUR DOG'S PAW WITH NONTOXIC,
WASHABLE PAINT IN YOUR FAVORITE COLOR AND
PRESS IT TO THE PAPER BELOW.

Remember the Time When...

USE THIS SPACE TO RECORD MEMORIES AND STORIES
THAT REVEAL YOUR DOG'S UNIQUE PERSONALITY
AND HIGHLIGHT THE KEY ROLE THEY PLAY IN YOUR FAMILY.

Add a photo of you and your incredible,
one-of-a-kind pup here:

MY SUNSHINE DOESN'T
COME FROM THE SKIES,
IT COMES FROM THE
LOVE IN MY DOG'S EYES.